They crawl. They creep.

They do not sleep.

Creepy, crawly bugs!

Bugs can fly.
They fill the sky.

Creepy, crawly bugs!

They have lots
of stripes and spots.

Creepy, crawly bugs!

Look in the corner.
Look in the crack.
Bugs are looking for a snack.

Creepy, crawly bugs!

6

Little bugs have little feet.
Creepy, crawly bugs are neat!

Creepy, crawly bugs!